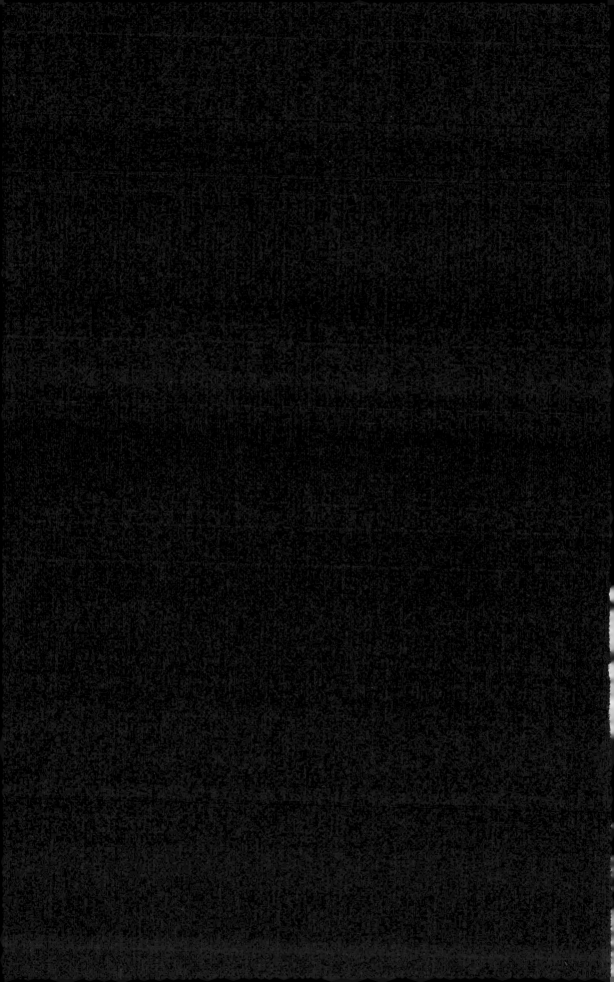

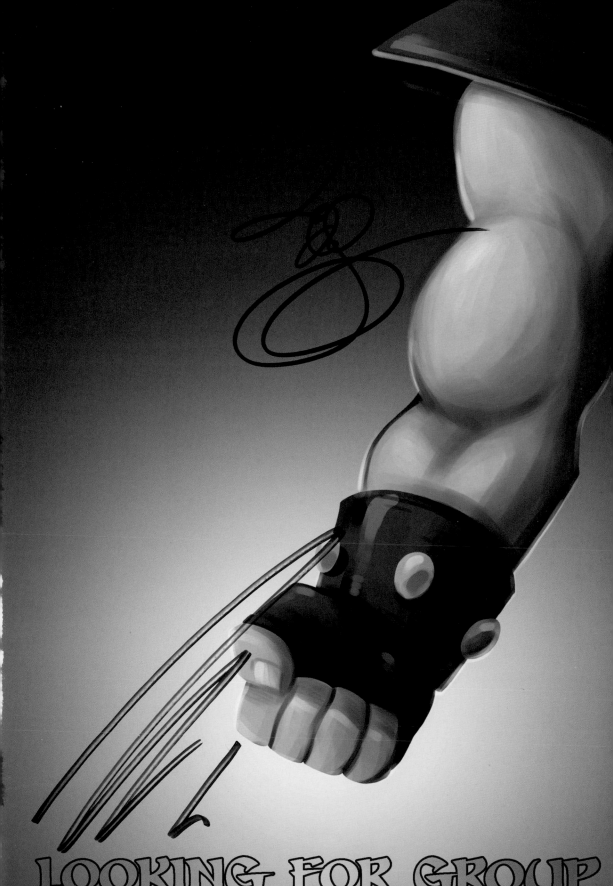

LOOKING FOR GROUP

VOLUME 4

Blind Ferret Entertainment presents:

LOOKING FOR GROUP

Volume 4

Ryan Sohmer
Writer

Lar deSouza
Artist

Randy Waxman
President & CEO

Ryan McCahan
Technical Director

Stuart Becker
Public Relations Manager

Rich Young
Business Development

Matthew Stone
Media Director

Fred Lawton
Accounting

Nick Di Feo
Sales Manager

www.lfgcomic.com

ISBN 978-1-926838-08-3

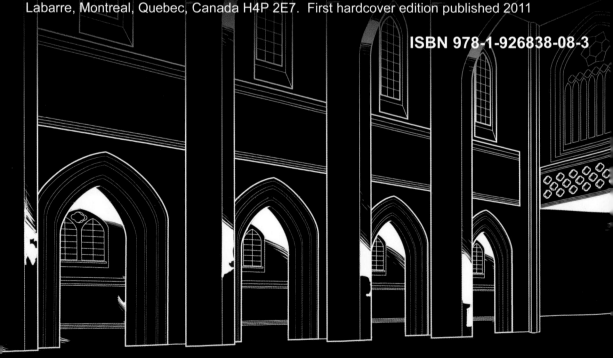

Foreword by
Joe Abercrombie

A tale is yet told, yet whispered – throatily – of a mystical land in which a battle was waged by good against evil. The epic story of a band of stalwart heroes, against which the tide of darkness broke like a reeking sea upon a dauntless bastion. The inspiring legend of a group of incorruptible champions who, through goodness, charity, comradeship and white clothing, laid low the army of chaos and stood triumphant, a shining example to all who would come after . . .

Looking For Group

Is not that story.

And yet it is no less classic a tale. For beneath the ready wit and the vivid artwork that strikes one in webcomic form, beneath the low laughs and the high drama, beneath the holy swords and unholy magics, the minotaur rages and head explosions, the yellow eyes and the green cleavage, in collected form one discerns a deeper, purer, more universal story.

For this is a tale of coming of age.

It is the story of a man (or, indeed, an elf, but you know what I mean) who learns, as must we all, to put aside childish things – in this case his inflexible attachments to truth, justice, honour and the protection of the innocent. The tale of a man (or elf) who graduates from a focus on the simply good to an appreciation of the greater good.

And, indeed, on occasion, the necessarily evil. The legend of a man (or elf) who reaches a sensible, adult compromise on minor concessions such as the slaughter of the helpless, alliance with the spawn of darkness, face melting and the eating of babies.

For in the end, no man (or, yes, elf) is an island. No one can stand alone against life's ups and downs. Or an evil empire. Especially not the evil empire, they always have big armies. And the cool uniforms. And sometimes dragons, battle-mages, and kinky dwarves. But I digress. My point is, whether we are in the business of traveling through time to restore a mystical kingdom or insurance adjustment, we all need friends, or at least companions. And we cannot always find the companions we would choose. We are all forced to make alliances, compromises, and occasionally sweet, sweet music with those that fate throws into our path, or to fail alone. And it is those compromises that make us better people. Even if they also occasionally shower us with gore. We all need something to be a part of.

In a most profound sense, are we not all . . . *looking for group* . . . ?

Joe Abercrombie
July, 2011

Joe Abercrombie is a Father, film editor, thirty-years a gamer of all kinds, and author of edgy yet amusing fantasy novels, The First Law, Best Served Cold, and The Heroes. The Heroes recently made #3 on the UK Hardcover bestseller list, and his First Law trilogy of books have sold over a million copies in more than twenty countries

BY RYAN SOHMER & LAR DESOUZA

ON YOUR WORD.

SOMETHING'S NOT RIGHT.

THEY'RE NOT MAKING THEIR WAY TO KETHENECIA.

YOU THINK THEY'RE SEARCHING BLINDLY?

NO.

I BELIEVE THEY'RE PATROLLING THE AREA.

ONLY ONE WAY TO FIND OUT.

STEAL THEIR SOULS,

KILL 'HEM AND IMBUE THEIR SPIRITS INTO AN AMUSING ANIMAL THAT I WILL TEACH TO SPEAK?

ARCHERS TO TRACK MY HANDS.

UNDERSTOOD.

HO THERE.

LOOKING FOR GROUP

BY RYAN SOHMER & LAR DESOUZA

HOW MUCH FURTHER?

WE'LL REACH CAMP BY SUNSET.

IT'S ONLY A FEW LEAGUES BEYOND THE KETHENECIAN WALL.

WHAT WALL?

YEP.

THAT'S DEFINITELY NEW.

WHAT ELSE HAS CHANGED DURING OUR ABSENCE?

MORE THAN I'D LIKE, I WAGER.

LOOKING FOR GROUP

BY RYAN SOHMER
& LAR DESOUZA

LOOKING FOR GROUP

BY RYAN SOHMER & LAR DESOUZA

MY LORD?

WAS IT WISE TO GIVE THE UNDEAD A PIECE OF KETHENECIAN SOIL?

THOSE UNDEAD WILL GO A LONG WAY TO KEEPING THIS CITY AND ITS PEOPLE SAFE.

BESIDES,

I'VE GIVEN THE PLOTS OF LAND SURROUNDING RICHARD'S TO VARIOUS RELIGIOUS GROUPS.

HOWDY, NEIGHBOR.

GET OFF MY LAWN.

LOOKING FOR
GROUP

BY RYAN SOHMER
& LAR DESOUZA

LOOKING FOR GROUP

BY RYAN SOHMER & LAR DESOUZA

THE FORTIFICATIONS LOOK GOOD.

THEY ARE.

YOUR CONFIDENCE IS INSPIRING.

THE FORTIFICATIONS AT BLOODRAGE AND THE GNOME MOUNTAIN ALSO LOOKED GOOD.

THOSE DIDN'T HOLD MY MEN OFF.

NEITHER WILL THESE SUFFICE TO HOLD OFF THE KING'S FLEET.

IF THAT'S THE CASE, YOU'RE TELLING ME WE'VE BEEN GATHERING PEOPLE TOGETHER SO THEY'LL BE EASIER TO SLAUGHTER?

NO.

I'VE HEARD IT SAID THIS CITY WAS PROTECTED.

BEFORE YOU CAME HERE.

THE SAND DRAGONS.

WE MIGHT THINK ABOUT ASKING THEM TO RETURN.

QUEST ACCEPTED.

LOOKING FOR GROUP

BY RYAN SOHMER & LAR DESOUZA

PLOOK

SHLUK

AND?

THERE'S A CAVERN DOWN THERE.

EXCELLENT.

MANY BOTHANS DIED TO BRING YOU THIS INFORMATION.

THEY'RE CALLED GNOMES

AND YOU KILLED THEM!

LOOKING FOR
GROUP

BY RYAN SOHMER
& LAR DESOUZA

GET UP.

WE NEED TO GO AFTER CALE.

DID YOU MISS THE PART WHERE HE GOT EATEN?

LET'S GO.

PATIENCE, GID.

PATIENCE.

THE ELF WILL BE BACK IN TWENTY-FOUR HOURS,

IN SOME FORM OR ANOTHER.

WE DON'T KNOW WHAT WE'RE RUNNING INTO DOWN HERE.

OR WHAT WE'RE STEPPING INTO.

STOP HELPING.

THE LAST THING WE WANT TO DO IS STEP IN A STEAMING PILE OF CALE.

LOOKING FOR GROUP

BY RYAN SOHMER
& LAR DESOUZA

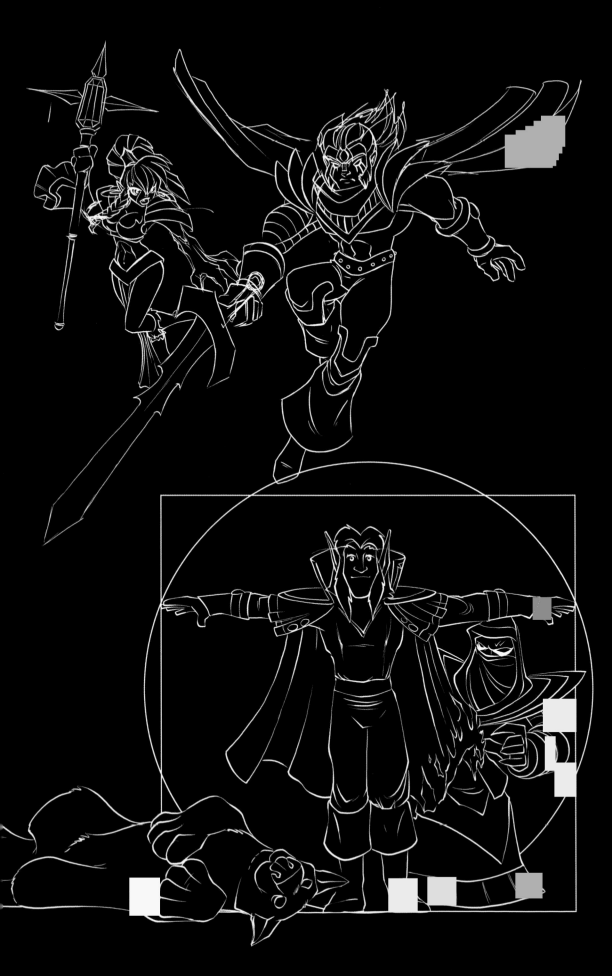

LOOKING FOR GROUP

BY RYAN SOHMER
& LAR DESOUZA

YOU'RE AWAKE.

GOOD.

I'M ALIVE?

I THOUGHT I WAS BEING EATEN.

BY LITTLE PEOPLE.

INSIDE A GIANT WORM.

THAT WAS ALSO EATING ME.

BUT SLOWER.

IT'S BEEN A ROUGH DAY FOR YOU.

BY RYAN SOHMER & LAR DESOUZA

NICE CATCH.

BY RYAN SOHMER & LAR DESOUZA

THIS IS MY ISSUE.

WITHOUT A DOUBT, I AM THE MOST POWERFUL WARLOCK THAT THIS WORLD OR ANY OTHER HAS SEEN IN EONS.

AND?

YOU'RE USING ME AS A MOUNT.

CONGRATULATIONS,

YOU'VE BEEN PROMOTED TO 'SHIELD'.

THANK YOU.

SHALL WE GO THANK THE LITTLE PEOPLE THAT MADE THIS ALL POSSIBLE?

I THINK WE SHALL.

RAAWWR

SBLORGSH

KRAK

WAAAASSSSSSUUUP?

SO WHASSUP, WARLOCK?

KILLING A BLARGH.,

KILLING A DRAGON.

TRUE,

TRUE.

BY RYAN SOHMER & LAR DESOUZA

YOU BETRAYED YOUR SWORN ALLEGIANCE TO YOUR KING.

A KING NO ONE HAS SEEN IN DECADES.

WHERE IS HE, AELLOON?

I WILL ASK THE QUESTIONS HERE, FATHER.

HOW DO YOU CHOOSE THESE TINY ABOMINATIONS OVER YOUR OWN PEOPLE?

SPEAK UP, FATHER.

SOME...

SOME OF THEM...

ARE LARGER THAN OTHERS.

LOOKING FOR GROUP

BY RYAN SOHMER & LAR DESOUZA

ARE YOU READY?

I THINK SO.

THEN TAKE A STEP, ELF.

IT'S OKAY.

WE'LL TRY AGAIN.

I'M JUST NOT CRAZY ABOUT HAVING AN AUDIENCE.

I LIKE IT WHEN HE FALLS.

LOOKING FOR GROUP

BY RYAN SOHMER & LAR DESOUZA

HAVEN'T SEEN YOU IN A WHILE, WARLOCK.

VERY OCCUPADO.

PRETEND YOU'RE OF AN ATTRACTIVE RACE FOR A MOMENT.

HNOOOOOOOGH!

WHOSE ORGANS?

SOME GUY NAMED SANTINO VALENTINO.

I ALSO TOOK HIS BOX OF ASSORTED CANDIES.

BY RYAN SOHMER & LAR DESOUZA

IT'S AN IMPRESSIVE TABLE.

ISN'T IT?

IT'S ROUND TO IMPLY THAT EVERYONE SEATED IS OF EQUAL RANK.

THIS IS MY SEAT.

THIS IS YOUR SEAT.

IT'S LITTLE TO IMPLY—

I KNOW WHAT IT IMPLIES.

LOOKING FOR GROUP

BY RYAN SOHMER & LAR DESOUZA

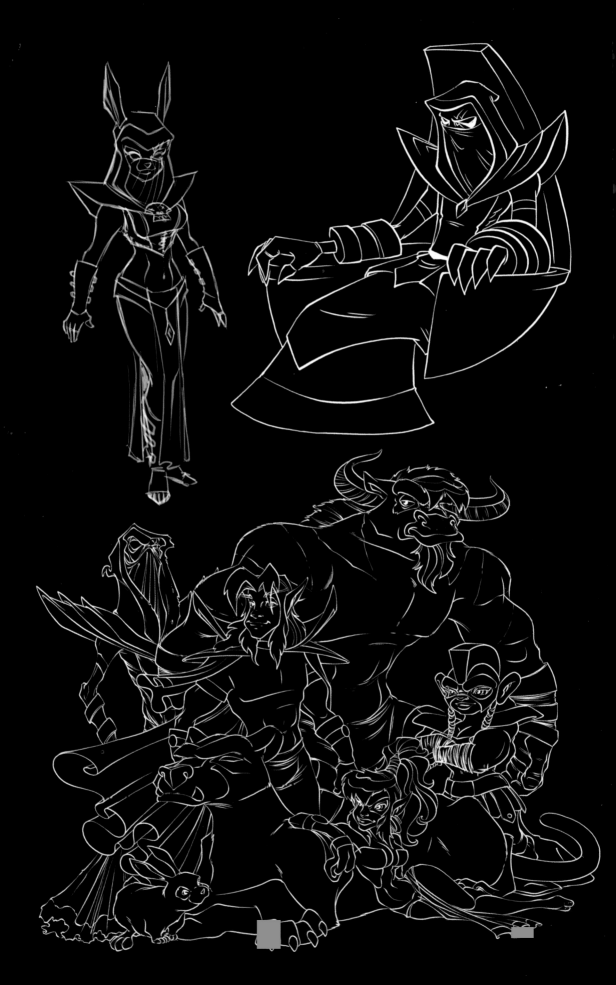